PROPHET SHEESH (A.S) (ALAIHI SALAM)

SEEMA SUHANA

Contents

Contents

Foreword

These books gives us knowledge about our beloved Prophets in story form . Books are available on all e-sites such as Amazon (India , USA , UK) , Flipkart (India) , Snapdeal (India) , Booktopia (UK,USA) , Barneandnoble(UK,USA) Shopee (India) ,wordery (USA) ,Wob (UK), Libro (USA) , Notionpress (India) , Mobythegreat (U.S) , Libroworld (U.S) , Powell's (City of Boos (U.S)) , Hugendubel.de (Germany) , Walmart (U.S) , Betterworldbooks (U.S) , Alibris (U.S) . contact me on instagram @Soulful_suhana to order in bulk and to get great discounts on it

(A.S)-Alaihi Salam

These books are available in English , Hindi , Roman Urdu

English :

Book 1 : Story of Prophet Adam (A.S)

Book 2: Prophet Sheesh (A.S)

Book 3: Prophet Idrees (A.S)

Book 4 :Strom of Prophet Nuh (A.S)

Book 5 : Journey from heaven to strom (Story of Prophet Adam (A.S) from heaven to Prophet Nuh (A.S) in floods and strom)

Roman Urdu

Book 1 : " Kahani Adam (A.S) Ki"

Book 2:"Hazrat Sheesh (A.S) "

Book 3: " Aknookh Yani Hazrat Idrees (A.S) "

Book 4 :"Toofan -e-Nuh "

(Story of Hazrat Nuh (A.S)"

Book 5 :"Arsh se Toofan Tak "

(Story of Hazrat Adam (A.S) in Jannah to Hazrat Nuh (A.S) In Floods And Strom)

Hindi

पुस्तक 1: पैगंबर आदम (अलैही सलाम) की कहानी

पुस्तक 2: पैगंबर शीश (अलैही सलाम)

पुस्तक 3: पैगंबर इदरीस (अलैही सलाम)

पुस्तक 4: पैगंबर नूह (अलैही सलाम) का तूफ़ान

पुस्तक 5: जन्नत से तूफ़ान तक

(पैगंबर आदम (अलैही सलाम) से पैगंबर नूह (अलैही सलाम) तक)

Acknowledgements

(A.S) Refers to Alaihi Salam

ALHAMDULLIAH FOR EVERYTHING

I also do Arabic calligraphy

Dm me to placed your customised order

Do follow me on

youtube channel: soulful suhana

instagram id : soulful_suhana

CHAPTER I

Prophet Adam (A.S) and Hawwa (A.S) in grieve

After the murder of Habeel, Hawwa (A.S) and Prophet Adam (A.S) used to be very sad, both of them were always in grief . Remembering Habeel, they used to weep all the time.

Prophet Adam (A.S) prayed to Allah : " O Allah , grant me child who is a believer of you and a help me in widening your religion in the world , and even after me he made sure your message is common in the world ".

CHAPTER II

Birth of Prophet Sheesh (A.S)

Both Prophet Adam (A.S) and Hawwa (A.S) were very sad about the murder of Habeel. they were always in grief and always prayed to Allah

Allah accepted the prayer of Prophet Adam (A.S) and Hawwa (A.S) and blessed him with a good noble son.

Prophet Adam (A.S) and Hawwa (A.S) were very happy with his birth.

Hawwa (A.S) named their beloved son Sheesh, which means "a beautiful gift from Allah ".

Prophet Sheesh (A.S) was much more beautiful and handsome than his father in terms of appearance and wisdom.

CHAPTER III

Upbringinng of Prophet Sheesh (A.S)

Hawwa (A.S) and Prophet Adam (A.S) loved Prophet Sheesh (A.S) very much.

Prophet Adam (A.S) kept Prophet Sheesh (A.S) with him all the time .

They have come to know that this child will be their successor to the survivors of their childrens.

Prophet Adam (A.S) and Hawwa (A.S) concentrated in upbringing trained him in education from the very beginning.

Prophet Adam (A.S) used to refer to Jannah stories to Prophet Sheesh (A.S) and show him the difference of good and sack .

As Prophet Sheesh (A.S) grew older, his hidden education and parental training continued to take colour.

Prophet Adam (A.S) used to tell Prophet Sheesh (A.S) about the day and night and taught him about the prayer to be offered that was during these times.

He also informed about Storm of Noah and what came later.

Prophet Adam (A.S) and Hawwa (A.S) had expectations from Prophet Sheesh (A.S) because one of their sons had been killed and the other went in the guidance of Shaitan.

Now, in order to fight for the religion of Allah , fight with shaitan, after Prophet Adam (A.S) Prophet Sheesh (A.S) was the only one successor and hope

Prophet Sheesh (A.S) learnt different things from Prophet Adam (A.S), but he could not get all the knowledge of Prophet Adam (A.S), as he learnt from Allah.

CHAPTER IV

The Real story worshiping statues

There were some good people between Prophet Adam (A.S) and Prophet Sheesh (A.S) and others used to praise them for their good deeds and follow them.

Budha was a noble person, and he was a very beloved person of his people. When he died, his people his follower would sit surrounded by his grave and wipe tears

When shaitan saw them, he came as a man in human form and said, "I saw you crying, so what do you think ? , I can and want to make a picture of Budh for you?"

you keep this picture of him in your assembly and remember him when you see it in your assembly.

They agreed with the Shaitan So he made a picture of this noble man.

followers said, "If we keep his picture , we will have more passion in our prayers ."

And they used to keep the picture of Budh in their assembly and offer their prayers

And when they died and the second generation came, the shaitan explained them that their ancestors were worshipping picture.

When shaitaan saw this scene, of people sitting in the assembly worshipping the picture, he said to them , " should I keep a Budh's statue in every house of yours."

They agreed to shaitan's word and every one of them kept budh's statue in one's house thus budh's was mentioned in every house.

Then their children were said same thing by shaitan and practiced same then next generations came , they forgot that budh was a Noble man.

They brought him to worship as God, and then they began to worship this god, denying

Allah . Thus the first one to be prayed was the Budh a noble man who later was called God Budh .

CHAPTER V

The Desire to Eat Jannah Fruit

When the time of the death of Prophet Adam (A.S) approached, he said to his children, "I heartly wish to eat the fruits of Paradise."

The fruits of paradise are and same like worldly fruits.

Apple , orange , pineapple etc all these fruits are present in paradise.

The difference between the fruits of paradise and the fruits of world is that the fruit of Jannah never gets rotten which is why they are never bad.

Similarly, fruits of the world are more temporary and the fruit of paradise are maintained.

Therefore, The Prophet Adam (A.S) wanted to eat the fruits of Paradise, and his sons went in search of Fruits

The Prophet Adam (A.S) said to his sons , "Go to Ka'bah and pray that Allah make my wish to eat fruit come true ."

after receiving order from father , Prophet Adam (A.S) son's took baskets and axe with them in search of fruits of paradise

They found Angel Jibrael(A.S) and other angels there, they had the shroud, fragrance, etc. of Prophet Adam (A.S).

Angel Jibrael (A.S) and other Angels, asked "What are Prophet Adam's children looking for ?" they replied and mentioned "Our father is a patient and ill and .his desire to eat fruit of Jannah.

Angels said, Come with us, we have brought with us the fruits of paradise.

Angels came in front of them in human form.

Angels said to Son's of Prophet Adam (A.S) , " Your father is nearing death ." nearly he dont have capacity to eat fruit

CHAPTER VI

Prophet Adam (A.S) commanded Prophet Sheesh (A.S) to pray for him

When Prophet Adam (A.S) fell ill, he wished to eat foods of Paradise he asked all his sons to get fruits of Paradise, a few sons went out in search of fruit towards forest, a few sons went out to Kaaba to pray that Allah grant them fruits of paradise so that their father's

wish could be fulfilled, but Prophet Sheesh (A.S) remained in the service of Prophet Adam (A.S).

When Prophet Adam's other sons who went to get fruit of Jannah and they failed to get fruits for him of Jannah

Then Prophet Adam (A.S) said to Prophet Sheesh (A.S) , " you go to Allah 's house kaaba and pray to Allah , and Allah will send me fruit with the blessings of your prayer " .

Prophet Sheesh (A.S) said: " you are my father , you are surely dear to him than me , you by praying Allah will surely send the fruit and your prayer will be accepted by Allah . "

On this Prophet Adam (A.S) said ," I am ashamed of the blessings of Allah for eating friut from tree in Jannah and you are clean ".

Prophet Sheesh (A.S) went there and prayed, and he saw That Angel Jibrael (A.S) was coming towards him with basket , and in this basket there was fruits and other dry fruits from Jannah, and another female angel hoor was appearing towards him by carrying basket on her head.

CHAPTER VII

Prophet Sheesh (A.S) married To Hoor

When a Female Angel hoor came with Angel Jibrael , Prophet Adam (A.S) asked Angel Jibrael (A.S) for whom this Female Angel hoor was for.

Angel Jibrael (A.S) said: "Allah has sent this hur from heaven to Prophet Sheesh (A.S) because all your children were born by Allah in pair of a girl and a boy, except for Prophet Sheesh (A.S) so this Hoor has sent it to Prophet Sheesh (A.S)

After that Prophet Adam (A.S) accepted this hoor and gave her to him in the provisions of Prophet Sheesh (A.S) .

The language of this hur was Arabic. The children of Prophet Sheesh (A.S) and hur also spoke Arabic

The Messenger of Allah Mohammed (peace and blessings of Allah be upon him) is also from the generation of Prophet Sheesh (A.S) and hoor

CHAPTER VIII

Advice from Prophet Adam (A.S)

At the time of Death of Prophet Adamapproached, he called his son Prophet Sheesh (A.S) near him.And he advised , " O my obedient son , you will be my successor . Do dhikr of Allah and whenever you mention Allah , do mention with him the name of his beloved Muhammad , I saw his name written on the Heaven at that time, when i was layered in the midst of the soul and the gritty

When I went round all the heavens, There he was, in all respects,

your glory in the Lord of Honour. I saw this word in which the name of Beloved Mohammed was there

when My Lord placed me in Paradise, I did not see a palace, any food, any window, any place where his name was not named, so you also mention them frequently.

CHAPTER IX

The Will of Prophet Adam (A.S)

Prophet Adam (A.S) made Prophet Sheesh (A.S) as his caliph and successor at the time of his death and said his will to him that when strom of nuh strikes in the time of nuh and If you are at that time Then you keep my bones in ship. who will be saved from being destroyed or asked your children to do so in your will

Prophet Adam (A.S) wrote his blessings and will in a book in which was the message of Allah and Haidayath.

Prophet Adam (A.S) asked to protect book from Kabeel and his children as they couldn't damage book, nor they could change the book.

Prophet Adam (A.S) advised his son Prophet Sheesh (A.S) five (5) things in his will And he said, "You should also give this advice to your children, and that is my will and blessings."

- *Do not rely on the world and on its life Allah did not like my being satisfied with Paradise and finally I had to leave.*

- *And do not follow women's wish blindly . I followed the woman's wish and fed fruit from the tree and regreted it later*

- *Think about the end of what you want to do first, if I had thought about the end, it would have been easy not with Hoordles in life*

- *Don't do when your heart is not satisfied with doing because my heart was not satisfied and was shaking at the time of eating fruit .*

- *Consult in your work because if I had consulted, I would not have been in difficult situation in the same way.*

CHAPTER X

The death of Prophet Adam (A.S)

Prophet Adam (A.S) made Prophet Sheesh (A.S) as his caliph and successor at the time of his death

Prophet Adam (A.S) the first human being and the first prophet, was also the first prophet to pass away from this world, after having lived for approx. thousand years.

Before his death, Prophet Adam (A.S) reassured his children that Allah would not leave man alone on earth but would sent His prophets to guide them. The prophets would have different names, traits and miracles but they would be united in one thing i-e the call to worship Allah alone. This was Prophet Adam's request to his children. Prophet Adam (A.S) finished speaking and closed his eyes. Then the Angels entered his room and surrounded him. When Prophet Adam (A.S) recognizes the Angle of Death among them, his heart smiled peacefully.

When the angels came to the take the soul of Prophet Adam (A.S) to be taken to Jannah . So Hawwa (A.S) recognized them.

She went near Prophet Adam (A.S) , cried aloud, and went to tight grip him.

The Prophet Adam (A.S) said, " get Separated from me. I had suffered because of you before, Get your hands on me and my Lord's Angels , then Angels took the soul of Prophet Adam (A.S), Gave them Ghusl, put on a shroud, smelled them , Dig the grave

Angels performed the funeral prayer of Prophet Adam (A.S) Then they brought Prophet Adam (A.S) body down to the grave. Put a fist on top of them

Prophet Sheesh (A.S) followed the words and methods of Angel Jibrael (A.S) to Burial Prophet Adam (A.S)

And then Angels said, "O Prophet Adam's sons , this is the way for you to do so." Then the people were not known by the command of burial.

They don't know how kabeel buried his brother , So the Angles were sent to tell them how the burial ceremonies should perform

So it was thus known how to bury man by Angels

The only sin Prophet Adam (A.S) did was to eat the fall of the tree in the life of 960.

According to different narrations, the day Prophet Adam (A.S) died was Friday.

A year after the death of Prophet Adam (A.S) , Hawwa (A.S) also died and was buried near him .

CHAPTER XI

Man in the world

All human beings in the world are children of Prophet Adam (A.S)

.Habeel was martyred at the age of 20 by his brother Kabeel . As Habeel was unmarried when he was martyred he did not have any child meanwhile another son Kabeel was disobedient of Allah and follower of Shaitan .

Later all the disobedients of Allah was killed in the strom of Prophet Nuh (A.S).

CHAPTER XII

Personality of Prophet Sheesh (A.S)

Prophet Sheesh (A.S) was alike of Prophet Adam (A.S). Prophet Sheesh (A.S) had 4 sons in which eldest was Anoosh , he became the successor of Prophet Sheesh (A.S). Prophet Sheesh (A.S) was on Prophecy duties . Prophet Sheesh (A.S) guided human beings after the death of Prophet Adam (A.S).

One of the features of Prophet Sheesh (A.S) is that man , is of his generation as Habeel was murdered and did not have any children

Kabeel's decendants (children) was later perished in Strom of Prophet Nuh (A.S) as they were disobedient of Allah and involved in sins like Adultery , Drunkenness, and Atheism.

Prophet Adam (A.S) was scared that Prophet Sheesh (A.S) will be martyed unlike kabeel , so Prophet Adam (A.S) ordered Prophet Sheesh (A.S) to keep his knowledge secretive from Kabeel and his children

Prophet Sheesh (A.S) invited the people to do good deeds. After becoming successor Prophet Sheesh (A.S), was also threatened by Kabeel.

CHAPTER XIII

Prophet Sheesh (A.S) on Prophethood

Allah blessed Prophet Sheesh (A.S) with Prophethood and blessed him with many children

The life of Prophet Sheesh (A.S) was declared in Mecca to spread faith of Allah among humans . During his prophethood, he had connections with Angel Jibrael (A.S) and other Angels

In Quran, there are 25 Prophets mention in which Prophet Sheesh (A.S) name is not included in hadith Prophet Sheesh (A.S) is mention being of Prophet.

Prophet Sheesh (A.S) childrens were very obedient and were engaged in religious activities with their father

Prophet Sheesh (A.S) spent his whole life according to teachings of his father . Due to declining age , Prophet Sheesh (A.S) children took all the responsibilities of him .

CHAPTER XIV

Saheefe (Pages)

Allah sent down 100 Saheefe and four (4) books on His Prophets Out of 100 Saheefe, 50 Saheefe were sent upon Prophet Sheesh (A.S).

CHAPTER XV

Prophet Sheesh (A.S) concern for the descendants (children) of Kabeel

Allah made Prophet Sheesh (A.S) an individual on the great scene of Prophethood and blessed him children.

Prophet Sheesh (A.S) children were very obedient and were engaged in religious activities with their father

Prophet Sheesh (A.S) spent his whole life according to teachings of his father . Due to declining age , Prophet Sheesh (A.S) children took all the responsibilities of him .

Prophet Sheesh (A.S) was worried about his brother Kabeel's children being tool of shaitan , being influenced by shaitan doing acts which involved in all kinds of sins.

Kabeel children started worshipping statues . They made statues of their father and other people

CHAPTER XVI

Jewish and Christian

Like Muslims, Jews and Christians also believe that Prophet Sheesh (A.S) is the son of Prophet Adam (A.S) and Hawwa (A.S) . They do believe in Prophecy of Prophet Sheesh (A.S)

CHAPTER XVII

Two different generations inhabited

The people were divided into two groups. Good people with Prophet Sheesh (A.S) and bad people with Kabeel. Prophet Sheesh (A.S) settled on land Kabeel was setteled in the mountains

At that time, two different generations were inhabited, i.e., one on the mountain and the other on the land .

Men in the mountains were handsome and charming while their women were brown in colour.

This was opposite on the land i.e., women were beautiful and men were dusky in colour

CHAPTER XVIII

Kabeel's descendants (children)

There was some time loosen for the punishment of the kabeel, so that he may repent and be on the way.

He went to the far-flung and settled in The Fold.

Khanook was born to kabeel

Then

Indar was born to khanook

Then

Mahaveel was born to Indar

Then

Matusheel was born to Mahaveel

Then

Lamik was born to Matusheel

Then

Aamaal named a boy was born to Lamik , a boy in the house of deeds, the first man to collect good wealth.

Then

Shatubaal was born to Amaal here in the works of the first man who performed tabla and sarangi yajat.

Then

Toh-Bel-Tin was born in shatubaal's house. Toh-Bel-Tin Worked on tambi and iron

Then

Naumi named girl was born to Toh-Bel-Tin

Similarly, the disobedient children of Prophet Adam (A.S) continued.

CHAPTER XIX

Spreading mischief, anarchy, mutiny, quarrel by descendants (children) of Kabeel

The descendants (children) of kabeel , who were settled on the mountain, started Spreading mischief, anarchy, mutiny, quarrel among themselves .

Sins like murder , mischief, anarchy, mutiny were common in their society . As the time passed by they started spreading those sinful acts in the society of Prophet sheesh (A.S)

CHAPTER XX

Shaitan began his work

Now Shaitan started his work. Shaitan came in the society of humans who lived land in human form , He became a servant of one person and stayed there to serve him.

He invented flute and started playing which had a very melodious sound which people had never heard before.

People got busy listening to him and used to sit around him just to listen melodious sound of flute

In a short time this news spread from door to door and people started visiting just to hear melodious sound.

Then they set aside a day in which all the people would be united would cherish their heart with evil device that Shaitan invented.

That day became the day of the festival and thousands of men and women began to gather just to entertain themselves . Shaitan used to entertain everyone , women used to dress beautifully and have conversations with non mahram men

Coincidentally, one day a man who lived in mountain also came there. When he saw the beautiful women of land , he went back and mentioned the beauty of women to men in the mountain

Now the people from the mountain frequently visited land and took part in the festival

In this way slowly slowly men and women from mountain and land started mixing with each other.Adultery was common and this was haram (not permissable) in the eyes of Prophet Sheesh (A.S)

Humans of land and mountain exchanged marriages of their children , which reflected in the number of good humans , they were disobediant of Allah and Prophet Sheesh (A.S)

Later these disobediant people were destroyed in strom of Prophet Nuh (A.S) . These disobediant people caused a riot on the ground because of their actions. Prophet Sheesh (A.S) explained to the people of his community to be on the right path and fear from Allah .Only Some people remained in the community of Prophet Sheesh (A.S).

Time passed and the descendants(children) of Prophet Adam (A.S) continued to flourish. New settlements and historical changes of life were made . Things began to grow. Prophet Sheesh (A.S) continued to perform deeds of his Prophency. Prevented people from going offspring , near kabeel's children who got involved in sinful acts.

CHAPTER XXI

last days of life

In later life Prophet Sheesh (A.S) became weaker and weaker, but Prophet Sheesh (A.S) obediant children continued Prophet Sheesh (A.S)'s work . Prophet Sheesh (A.S) lived 912 in this world . Prophet Sheesh (A.S) spent his entire life in the teachings of his father .

CHAPTER XXII

Advice of Prophet Sheesh (A.S)

Prophet Sheesh (A.S) often said pious muslim is the one who has following qualities

1. Getting to know Allah

2. Knowing the good and the bad one

3. Obey the time who is the king himself

4.rights of parents and serve them

5. Performing good deeds and humanity for people.

6. Don't escalate one's anger

7. Helping and giving charity to required one

8.Refrain from sins ., on be patient and thankful in pain and Troubles

9. Treats needy correctly

10. Be patient when you suffer

11. Be thankful on Allah's blessing

CHAPTER XXIII

Death

According to some scholars, Prophet Sheesh (A.S) passed away in Makkah.

Prophet Sheesh (A.S) died at the age of 912 years. When the time of death of Prophet Sheesh (A.S) approached, he informed his son Anoosh of all matters.

Qinan became successor after Anoosh

After Qinan , Mahlaai became successor

After Mahlaai , Yarid became successor

After Yarid , khanook became successor

After Khanook ,Aknookh became successor . Aknookh is none other than Prophet Idrees (A.S)

After Prophet Sheesh (A.S) , prophecy was given to Prophet Idrees (A.S)

ANOOSH

↓

Qinan

↓

Mahlaai

↓

Yarid

↓

Kanook

↓

Aknookh(Prophet Idrees(A.S))

CHAPTER XXIV

Tomb of Prophet Sheesh (A.S)

Prophet Sheesh (A.S) was buried near his father.

Scholars say that at the time of the flood of Prophet Nooh(A.S), Prophet Nooh(A.S) took out the blessed body of Prophet Sheesh (A.S) and Prophet Adam (A.S) and placed inside ship.

After the flood ended placed their blessed body near Baitul Mamoor (Kaaba)

CHAPTER XXV

Descendants (children) of Prophet Sheesh (A.S)

Anush was born to Prophet Sheesh (A.S)

Prophet Sheesh (A.S) was 112 when Anush was born and Prophet Sheesh (A.S) lived 800 years and to Anush more boys and girls were born

kanan was born to Anush at that time Anush was 90 years old and after that Anush lived for 815 years. They were more birth of boys and girls.

When Kanan was 70 years old,in his house was born in Mehlael and after that Kanan lived for 40 years. They were more birth of boys and girls.

When Mehlael was was 65 years old, in their house Yarid was born, and after that, Mehlael lived for 830 years, and their was more birth of boys and girls.

When Yarid was 162, khanook was born , after which Yarid lived for 800 years. and after that, Mehlael lived for 830 years, and their was more birth of boys and girls.

When Khanook was 65 years old, in his house mattoshalak was born, after which Khanook lived for 800 years. They were more birth of boys and girls.

When Mattoshalak was 187 years old, in his house Lamic was born , after which Mattoshalak lived for 782 years. They were more birth of boys and girls.

When Lamic was 182, Prophet Noah (A.S) was born to him. He lived for nearly 1,000 years. They were more birth of boys and girls.

When Prophet Noah (A.S) was 500, Sam Ham Yafiz was born to him.

CHAPTER XXVI

Incidents that occured from Prophet Sheesh (A.S) to Yarid

Mahlaai was the one who established justice and his rule lasted for 40 years.

During his rule different tribes with their borders came into existence . He also made a magnificent crown for himself. He enjoyed wearning crown and ruled his kingdom.

- *Ajmi people thought these people was king of 60 tribes*
- *They defeated the army of Iblees and was so strict with them that they ran in the valley of the mountains.*
- *Killed disobedient and rebellious jinns*
- *Mahlaai is the first person who cut forest , settled city , build castle , laid the*

foundation and built Masjid.

- *Expanded city Saoos*

- *Babul city was built and expanded*

- *The first one to extract and began iron works And many weapons were made from it*

- *Built dams and collected water so People became interested in cultivation and agriculture .*

- *Killed Dangerous animals and made garments and mats from their skins*

After Mahlaai , his successor became his son Yarid, following his father's footsteps.

After Yarid, Aknookh became Yarid's successor . Aknookh is none other than Prophet Idrees (A.S)

After Prophet Adam (A.S), Prophet Idrees (A.S) was declared as Prophet by Allah.

CHAPTER XXVII

Aknookh none other than Prophet Idrees (A.S)

Aknookh is none other than Prophet Idrees (A.S). After Prophet Adam (A.S), Prophet Idrees (A.S) was declared as Prophet by Allah.

9 798887 838755

Printed by Libri Plureos GmbH in Hamburg,
Germany